Re'

"Women NEED this book! The honesty, transparency, and relatability will set women free! This devotional will take women on a journey that leads to freedom, healing, and transformation. It is a blueprint to a breakthrough."

—Whitney J. Hogans, Author, Singer, Songwriter, Speaker, and Educator

"*31 Days Towards The Reconstruction of a Virtuous Woman* will encourage young women to grow closer to God. The text is easy to read, it gives an awesome message without being to drawn out, and it captures your attention. It's like you're talking with your homegirl about God!"

—Dominique Obichere, Makeup Artist

"*31 Days Towards The Reconstruction of a Virtuous Woman* is a powerful devotional that allows you to realize that you are indeed worthy and can become the virtuous woman that God intends you to be. I enjoyed how the book guides us through our role of virtuosity through modern day references. It speaks to and navigates us through modern day questions, situations, reflections, and experiences."

—Brandi Brehon, Program Manager

"This book seems to help young women grow closer to God by providing a practical, scripture-based framework for understanding and embodying virtue in the modern world. It addresses the struggle for identity, which encourages readers to find strength and value in their faith and personal journey."

—Bryce Lennon, Content Creator

31 DAYS
TOWARDS THE
RECONSTRUCTION
OF A

A Devotional Journal

TRISTIAN HOLLEY

ELOHAI
INTERNATIONAL
PUBLISHING & MEDIA

Published by ELOHAI International Publishing & Media
P.O. Box 1883
Cypress, TX 77410
hello@elohaiintl.com
ElohaiIntl.com

ISBN: 978-1-953535-85-6

Library of Congress Control Number: 2024907989

Printed in the United States of America

Dedication

This devotional journal is dedicated to my daughters, Janiyah and Jurnee. I pray that you become the virtuous women that God intended you to be. And to my son, Isaiah—I strive to be the kind of woman he will proudly brag about to his friends in the future. I also dedicate this to my husband, Jeffery, for seeing me unconditionally, as Christ does. I love you for that! To my family, especially my cousin Bryce, who always reminded me about this crazy idea when we were in college: I did it, Bryce! Mommy, I love you and miss you so much! My prayer is to make you proud. I want you to know your child spread the good news and hope to this world. See you in heaven!

Lastly, to my queens, both young and old: When you read Proverbs 31:10–31, don't be intimidated by her, because that is *you*! That is you from the womb to your ugly truths to now. We are the virtuous women that God intended us to be. We just have to believe it!

Table of Contents

Introduction

In 2008, my senior year at *the* Elizabeth City State University, I was a part of the on-campus ministries, and we were planning a women's revival. When we discussed what the theme should be for the event, we couldn't think of anything, and we ended the meeting without knowing the theme. During that time, I was also a part of the Student Activities Committee. I created the entire theme for homecoming prior and started thinking about our Viking Fest theme in the spring. Creating themes was my thing.

But this theme was different. It described a woman's journey of walking with God. I struggled with this theme because I couldn't put it into words. I went to Scripture for inspiration and stumbled on Proverbs 31:10–31. I was twenty-one at the time. I was indeed the "Church Girl" that Beyoncé referred to in her song and still am in some ways. My walk with God was a little gray, or what some Christians call "lukewarm." But there was this constant pursuit of God—His pursuit as well—that kept us connected even when I was doing wrong.

So I was reading the scripture and immediately felt defeated. I said to myself, "This is not me!" I was reading it thinking, *I'm going to HELL! This doesn't describe me at all, but I have the pursuit and reverence of God. So why can't I be her?* I remember hearing God clearly say, "You *are* her. You just need to reconstruct her." Then the title, *The Reconstruction of a Virtuous Woman* came, and that was the theme for the revival. It was an awesome experience seeing young women worship like that on a college campus.

In 2012, I was twenty-six years old! I was at the point of no return in my life. I had put myself in pits no one could get me out of. I was broken—mentally, physically, and spiritually. The closest depiction was me walking toward the devil with his arms out, saying, "You have arrived!" As I reached for his hand, the softest voice said, "I can heal your broken heart. For who can find a virtuous woman? That answer is me!" In my moment of darkness and despair, suddenly there was light and optimism like no other. It was at that point I rededicated myself to the Lord. I pissed the devil off that day.

Now, a decade later, I'm thirty-six years old. I'm a wife and mother, and I keep asking myself, "Am I still the virtuous woman God intended me to be?" The answer is always YES! The interesting part of my journey is that people would come to me and say I did a complete one-eighty. They would say, "With your life several years ago, I couldn't picture where it is today." I always respond, "Neither could I. I never prayed for anything like this, but I know it was God who changed my life." I knew that God's transformative power did something to me, and today I believe I was and still am a virtuous woman, just remixed.

When we read the passage of the virtuous woman, we automatically think of the perfect woman. But when we compare her to the lives of women today, it almost appears that the virtuous woman is non-existent. In this lust-filled, "sexploitative" society, where women compare themselves to what they see on television, social media, woman-to-woman interactions, and not to mention the views of MEN, the question that needs to be asked is, "Who can find a virtuous woman? Is she still out there?" The answer is yes! She has to believe it, and the person who can truly answer that is God.

God Himself is the answer. Christ, as the architect, has shown us the blueprint through the Proverbs 31 woman (Proverbs 31:10–31) and how to live our lives victoriously—even after our past indiscretions. The reconstruction of a virtuous woman can be defined as every woman rediscovering herself through the lens of her Creator. Learning and unlearning truths about themselves could be the process of reconstructing their lives to be the virtuous women that God destined them to be.

I will sum up the past fourteen years of my life experiences in a thirty-one-day devotional demonstrating how to reconstruct your life into that of the virtuous woman God wants you to be! For some, it can take thirty-one days or longer. My reconstruction is still pending. But what a joy it is to be on a ride with someone who has always loved you unconditionally—God.

I'm honored that our paths have crossed and that we get to embark on this journey of holiness together. This devotional revolves around five principles that I believe have helped me cover (and reconstruct) every aspect of my life:

- Self-Worth
- Faith
- Beauty and Health
- Time and Purpose
- Nurturing Relationships

As the days progress, you will move into areas of your life where you will understand what God has to say about you and what your life should look like if you reflect in a godly manner. Each daily devotion has four pillars:

- Scripture
- Virtue of the Day
- Journal Prompt
- Virtuous Prayer

The SOAP Bible study method helped me on my journey; SOAP stands for Scripture, Observation, Application, and Prayer. I strongly recommend you try this. For my beginners, The Message Bible has done wonders in my life. It is easy for me to understand, but ultimately, you should use what works best for you! It's best to study with multiple Bible translations.

A disclaimer: As you already know, I like themes! Some of my titles are from songs I listened to along my journey. As you read along, you'll notice I'm a big R&B fan but mostly a Destiny's Child and Beyoncé fan. In fact, the theme song for this devotional is Destiny Child's "Have Your Way." You must be a true fan to know that song! This song was the soundtrack to my spiritual walk with God. All the emotions, backsliding, condemnation, yearning for God, and the fight to not give up were in this song. As a baby in Christ at the time, I listened to worship music that helped me in my walk. To be honest, my journey from secular to gospel has been up and down. However, when you are at the point of no return, it changes, and that is where I am. In the words of Jackie Hill Perry, "for the saints and ain'ts"—if this is too much for you, I understand, but this is for the ain'ts (both saved and unsaved).

Are you ready? The fact that you've decided to do this makes you dope, amazing, blessed, valued, and loved! You are a virtuous woman! Say that every day in the mirror until it is manifested outwardly. "You ready, T? Let's go get 'em!"

Principle #1: Self-Worth

A wife of noble character who can find?
She is worth far more than rubies.
Proverbs 31:10 (NIV)

The definition of worth means the value equivalent of someone or something under consideration; the level at which someone or something deserves to be valued or rated. In the Bible, rubies are mentioned several times. Isaiah 54:12 implies that rubies are expensive and highly desired. Rihanna should have changed her song from *Diamonds to Rubies* "Shine Bright Like a Ruby!" Now, if I'm reading this text right, (insert your name) is worth far more than rubies. Say it again! Say it out loud! Repeat it until it resonates in your spirit! Listen, this is just the first verse, and that should already give you the confidence to know that God sees your worth as higher than rubies, money, Prada, Gucci, Beamer, Benz, or Bentley. You name it, and you are above that! He looks at you with high standards. So why don't you feel that way about yourself? My prayer for the next five days is for you to seek validation from the Holy Spirit. When a negative thought starts to creep in (because it will), go back to this verse and cast it down. Shine bright, girl!

Day 1

Good Morning, Gorgeous!

Therefore, if anyone is in Christ, the new creation
has come: The old has gone, the new is here!
2 Corinthians 5:17 (NIV)

We know that baptism is the outward symbol of commitment to Christ. I was baptized at ten years old when I received Christ as my personal Savior. There's something about coming out of the water as a new person. You feel transformed from the inside out. Each day, I try to live out that new life. Have you heard the scripture that says, "The righteous falls seven times and rises again..."? Let's just say I had to recommit myself a couple of times. I got baptized again at twenty-three and at twenty-seven years old. Honestly, I feel like I'm due for another one.

I realized that water represented purification, sanctification, and renewal of spirit. Instead of these being moments of my life, I should have this attitude and sense of newness every day. I understand that God gives us new mercies each day when we open our eyes and take a breath from our night's rest. There is a newness, a sense of hope, or even an opportunity to do something different from yesterday.

The Bible says in Lamentations 3:22–24 (ESV), "The steadfast love of the LORD never ceases; his mercies never come to an end; they are new every morning; great is your faithfulness. 'The LORD is my portion,' says my soul, 'therefore I will hope in him.'" Hebrews 8:12 (ESV) states, "For I will be merciful toward their

3

iniquities, and I will remember their sins no more." God is not dwelling on the things from the past or even yesterday. He forgets them and gives us a new opportunity to get closer to Him or a new day to turn away from things that keep us apart from Him. When I think about it, I thank God that He is not like us.

I know for me; I fell victim to bringing my past into my future. God forgot all about it, but I was still sitting miserable. I read this devotion on new mercies, and I encourage everyone to try the "Fresh Start Effect": Every morning, when you wake up, have a new perspective. Envision God telling you that your mistakes, the way you act, and your mindset from yesterday are behind you. You have a clean slate this morning.

Journal Prompt: You have been given a clean slate today. How will you tackle the day pertaining to your thoughts and actions?

Virtuous Prayer: Heavenly Father, thank you for waking us this morning and giving us new mercies each day. Father, thank you for giving us a fresh start. Psalm 30:5 says, "Weeping may endure for a night, but a shout of joy comes in the morning." We thank you, Father, for giving us a clean slate. You gave us a clean slate when your Son died on the cross for our sins. He allows us to do better and be better, and we thank you, Lord. We thank you for giving us another day on this earth, for there were others who did not receive that, so we live our lives with purpose and mission because you give us the breath to do so. Lord, forgive our sins because to get a fresh start, we must acknowledge our shortcomings to you. Thank you, God, because once we confess, you remember no more and walk us through a new day with a fresh anointing. Again, we thank you for being with us.

_____

_____

_____

_____

_____

_____

_____

_____

_____

_____

_____

_____

_____

_____

_____

_____

_____

_____

_____

_____

_____

_____

_____

_____

Day 2
God's Craftmanship Was...
and Still Is Me!

For you created my inmost being;
you knit me together in my mother's womb.
I praise you because I am fearfully and wonderfully made;
your works are wonderful,
I know that full well.
My frame was not hidden from you
when I was made in the secret place,
when I was woven together in the depths of the earth.
Psalm 139:13–15 (NIV)

I always say if you have questions about *you*, go to the source! If you want to know why you were created, ask the Creator Himself. When I was in the pits back in 2013, I remember asking him, "Why was I created?" His answer was simple and true to who I am. He said, "I need another creative like me." I laughed it off, but that was indeed who I am. Whether seen or unseen, I have created a lot of ideas in my lifetime. At a younger age, I was fascinated with movies and music videos. I always said I wanted to be the female version of Hype Williams. I wrote screenplays. I assisted in live productions. I was that girl! However, during that time, I wasn't creating anything. I was simply going to work and existing. I lived for the weekends and partied all the time. It got to a point where I was unrecognizable to myself.

I was also guilty of being born out of wedlock. I thought God liked me but did not fully love me because I didn't enter the way He intended me to. I still sometimes feel that way with my daughter being born the same way. However, reading this scripture showed that I was crafted out of love. God knew everything about me and still deemed that I would enter this earth. It was the understanding that God, in His grace, took an interest in me before I was even born that transformed my thinking and revelation about this issue. My feelings were not accurate. The truth is that God loves me no less than He would if I were born within the confines of marriage. Grace causes Him to continue to pursue me, and I continue to have the desire for Him. Nothing about me is hidden from Him. God is omnipotent, omniscient, and omnipresent. He has all the answers about us. Your DNA is wrapped in the lineage of the most royal priesthood. So what better way of rediscovering yourself than by asking the Creator himself?

Journal Prompt: What are some questions that you want to ask God about yourself?

Virtuous Prayer: Father God, thank you for making everyone reading this beautiful and unique, crafted to be fearfully and wonderfully made. Lord, I thank you for making us so different because in everyone, there is a God-given gift that was strictly designed just for them. I pray that you reveal it to them and they know they are here for a reason. May we all confess God's craftmanship was...and still is me!

_____

_____

_____

_____

_____

_____

_____

_____

_____

_____

_____

_____

_____

_____

_____

_____

_____

_____

_____

_____

_____

_____

_____

_____

_____

Day 3

I Am a Love Song!

The Eternal your God is standing right here among you,
and He is the champion who will rescue you.
He will joyfully celebrate over you;
He will rest in His love for you;
He will joyfully sing because of you like a new husband.
Zephaniah 3:17 (The Voice)

Music is the soundtrack to our lives. Music is so influential and is like a virus that is highly infectious. Whether it is the catchy lyrics or the banging beat, music captivates our minds, bodies, and souls. On this third day, I want to take this time to not only celebrate you but serenade you with a song. The artist who is here to perform is well-renowned gospel extraordinaire...Jesus!

I know you all are reading this like "Huh?" But yes, Jesus is my favorite artist right now. Do you want to know why? Because Jesus is singing in heaven about me. When I read this verse, I said, "ME! He is singing about me!" In the Voice translation, it says, "He will joyfully sing because of you like a new husband." I think every girl's dream is to be serenaded by her man. I know mine is because my husband can actually sing.

As broken and lost as I was, I read that verse believing if no one was celebrating or praising me in the natural, I could know someone was praising me in the supernatural. Reading this verse gave me the confidence to move past my discretions because someone was cheering for me to succeed and was also going to help me reclaim my time! Seeing those words resonated in my spirit that there was somebody who loved me more than I loved myself, and I was curious to see why He loved me the way He did. I encourage you to love yourself because you have a fan singing your name from above.

Journal Prompt: What would be the title of Jesus' love song for you?

Virtuous Prayer: Father God, thank you for serenading me with your Word! Thank you for singing your praise when I couldn't sing it for myself. I want to sing your name all the days of my life. I will always and forever be your number one fan.

_____

_____

_____

_____

_____

_____

_____

_____

_____

_____

_____

_____

_____

_____

_____

_____

_____

_____

_____

_____

_____

_____

_____

_____

_____

_____

_____

_____

_____

_____

_____

_____

_____

_____

_____

_____

_____

_____

_____

_____

_____

_____

_____

_____

_____

Day 4
Flaws and All

You are altogether beautiful, my darling.
There is no flaw in you.
Song of Solomon 4:7 (NIV)

One of the quality traits I still can't wrap my brain around when it comes to God is His unconditional love for me. Sometimes I sit in awe trying to figure out why this person loves me! Nowadays, we would say, "The level of toxicity is too much to be around." But here we are. He chooses us every single time. I understand that by choosing me, simultaneously, I am choosing Him. It's just insane. I constantly think about Jesus choosing to die for a chick He never met. The level of gangster Jesus had—I honestly don't think any man can. *I'm going to take a bullet for my enemies!* "I think not!" It's hard to comprehend the caliber of love He has for us and that in His eyes, there is no flaw in you. I cry every time! All the evil things that people or even you have said about yourself...God sees that you have no flaw. When you receive Him, you are considered spotless. That is why I love these lyrics in "Flaws and All" by Beyoncé:

> I don't know why you love me
> And that's why I love you
> You catch me when I fall
> Accept me flaws and all
> And that's why I love you

I will forever hasten to His throne because I know His love is like no other and I can go to Him without condemnation. Jesus is Planet Fitness: a no-judgment zone! So today, walk in the truth that there is no flaw when you are in Christ Jesus.

Journal Prompt: What flaws have prevented you from fully embracing the love of God?

Virtuous Prayer: Father God, thank you for loving me the way you do. You love me, and you accept me—flaws and all. For that, I give my life to you. I pray to understand that, through you, there are no flaws in me. Thank you for your words!

_____

_____

_____

_____

_____

_____

_____

_____

_____

_____

_____

_____

_____

_____

_____

_____

_____

_____

_____

_____

_____

_____

_____

_____

_____

_____

_____

_____

_____

_____

_____

_____

_____

_____

_____

_____

_____

_____

_____

_____

_____

_____

_____

_____

Day 5
Hey, Queen!

But you are a chosen people, a royal priesthood, a holy nation,
God's special possession, that you may declare the praises of
him who called you out of darkness into his wonderful light.

1 Peter 2:9 (NIV)

My husband will always tell me that I'm a queen, and every
time we step out, we are representing royalty. My husband
takes pride in himself in how he looks and how he carries himself. He is a true king in the Holley household. Even before we
got married, he would always tell me I was a queen! His level of
confidence was always infectious because I never valued myself
in that light. Now I try to match his fly.

This is no different from being connected to God. You're trying to match His fly, right? The scripture says we are a *chosen*
people. What I like is that we are "God's special possession." By
reading this text, we understand that when we come under the
authority of God, we are a part of a lineage of royalty. We are connected to Jesus. For me, I understand that I'm connecting to the
King who dwells on this earth, performed miracles, and saved
mankind from itself. Not to mention, I have full access to talk to
Him anytime I feel like it. That should give you a level of flex!

Understanding that you're a part of that resurrecting power
should boost your self-esteem. It should help you understand your
value. Not only that but it also gives you a sense of responsibility.
First Corinthians 7:23 (TLB) says, "You have been bought and paid

for by Christ, so you belong to him." The cross proves your value, which makes it your responsibility to not only hold yourself to a standard but also share the good news with people while you're here. We are going to get into purpose later, so for now, know you are a queen! Hold your head up high, adjust your crown, and be the queen God destined you to be. It is your birthright!

Journal Prompt: Do you know who you are in Christ?

Virtuous Prayer: Father God, thank you for choosing me. Thank you that when I accepted Christ as my personal Savior, I was automatically added to the lineage of royalty. I am different; I no longer walk and talk the same, for I am made new in Christ. I pray that when I am down and out, you will remind me who I am and who I represent.

_____

_____

_____

_____

_____

_____

_____

_____

_____

_____

_____

_____

_____

_____

_____

_____

_____

_____

_____

_____

_____

_____

_____

_____

_____

_____

_____

_____

_____

_____

_____

_____

_____

_____

_____

_____

_____

_____

_____

_____

Principle #2: Faith

Charm is deceptive, and beauty is fleeting;
but a woman who fears the LORD is to be praised.
Proverbs 31:30 (NIV)

'm so proud of you! You have completed the first principle of self-worth. You are starting to feel good about yourself. This may have been an introduction or reintroduction to God. The lines of communication are open, and now, my sisters, it is time for you to go deeper within yourself.

In my journey, this was the hardest part—and still is the hardest part—of reconstructing myself into that virtuous woman. Like the "Versus" battle, it is your flesh versus spirit. To gain true faith in the Lord, it starts with the shedding of yourself. When I was young, this one simple verse stuck with me and still does today: Hebrews 9:22 (KJV) says, "And almost all things are by the law purged with blood; and without shedding of blood is no remission." We all know the redemption of humanity is through the shedding of Jesus' blood. When you have made up your mind that you can no longer straddle the fence or put yourself in condemnation, it is time to go through a sanctification process. To be sanctified is to be set apart, and human beings cannot sanctify themselves. The Triune God sanctifies them. So over the next five days, be prepared to confront the good, the bad, and the ugly of yourself. But just know, there is light on the other side of the tunnel. See you on the other side.

Day 6
Me, Myself, and I

Examine yourselves to see whether you are in the faith;
test yourselves. Do you not realize that Christ Jesus is in you—
unless, of course, you fail the test?
2 Corinthians 13:5 (NIV)

If we confess our sins, he is faithful and just and will
forgive us our sins and purify us from all unrighteousness.
1 John 1:9 (NIV)

Search me, God, and know my heart;
test me and know my anxious thoughts.
See if there is any offensive way in me,
and lead me in the way everlasting.
Psalm 139:23–24 (NIV)

Throughout my journey, God has pointed out certain books regarding specific areas of my life. I encourage everyone to read *Dangerous Prayers: Because Following Jesus was Never Meant to Be* Safe by Craig Groeschel. This book changed my life! The premise of the book is getting out of your comfort zone by praying boldly and honestly. It's about praying prayers that will automatically move the heart of God. Today I want to share one of the dangerous prayers with you.

After reading the scriptures of the day, God is trying to propel you to new heights, and for Him to do that, He has to make you uncomfortable. I love how Groeschel explains it in the book: "Instead of indulging our daily desires, He calls us to deny them for something eternal." My prayer is for everyone to be the best version of themselves and true representatives of Christ. I challenge each one of you to confront the negatives in your life. What are some of the ugly truths about you? What are some things you don't want people to know about you? Give yourself a sin inventory.

An ugly truth about me: I used to wish evil on people who had hurt me in the past. I carried a lot of unforgiveness in my heart. I would celebrate their downfall. I wanted to share that because when you ask God to search your heart, He will reveal the worst—but thank God He is not like us. If He was like us, He would've cut me off, saying I was trifling. Instead, He loved me and told me the energy I put out there was going to come right back. He had a better plan for me. He told me to repent and, instead of cursing them, pray for them. At that moment, because I was so desperate for God and change, I started praying for my ex and his marriage. I started praying for him to prosper. I got uncomfortable.

I went from praying for an ex in 2012 and then, by February 2013, I was tired of praying for him and wanted to start praying for others. I started putting up Facebook posts asking people if I could pray for them. My heart, which had been consumed with hate and envy, turned into a heart of love, compassion, and empathy. A chick who had been celebrating someone's downfall now wanted everybody to win.

So here I am over ten years later writing this devotional, asking God to search my heart and lead me in the right direction because I want Him to do extraordinary things in my life. I want to lead souls to Him through my testimony. This might take some time; it doesn't happen overnight. So today I ask you to take my challenge and ask God to search your heart. Get uncomfortable with yourself, and dive into the depths of your soul.

Journal Prompt: What are some ugly truths you don't want people to know about you?

Virtuous Prayer: Lord, search my heart and reveal my ugly truths. Lord, show me my past and present so I can break any strongholds that would keep me in a negative cycle or behavior. Assess my heart, Lord; reveal my fears, and uncover my sins. Father, forgive me, and change me from the inside out.

_____

_____

_____

_____

_____

_____

_____

_____

_____

_____

_____

_____

_____

_____

_____

_____

_____

_____

_____

_____

_____

_____

_____

_____

_____

_____

_____

_____

_____

_____

_____

_____

_____

_____

_____

_____

_____

_____

_____

_____

_____

_____

_____

_____

Day 7

Stripped

I have been crucified with Christ and I no longer live, but Christ
lives in me. The life I now live in the body, I live by faith in the
Son of God, who loved me and gave himself for me.
Galatians 2:20 (NIV)

By the seventh day God had finished the work he had been doing;
so on the seventh day he rested from all his work.
Genesis 2:2 (NIV)

You've made it to day seven. The number seven is a sign of
completion. God created everything in six days. On the seventh day, He rested. You should do the same. How are you feeling? I don't know about you, but a lot of weight was lifted off me when I decided to rest. I felt I was renewed by God.

The reconstruction of a virtuous woman has just begun. As I mentioned before, the Bible talks about dying to yourself daily. Always do a sin inventory within yourself. That's important to your self-care. For me, it is my sense of humility that I need God in my life every single day. Every day, I'm at His feet. Today, rest and celebrate the new you.

Journal Prompt: Over the last seven days, what has God revealed to you about yourself?

Virtuous Prayer: Lord, thank you for stripping me down to the pure nakedness of my soul. Thank you for allowing me to be reconstructed to the latest version of myself, which is rooted in you. I'm excited about the journey we are embarking on together. I pray that along my journey, you will remind me of the good, bad, and ugly that always keep me positioned at your feet. I am nothing without you. Amen!

_____

_____

_____

_____

_____

_____

_____

_____

_____

_____

_____

_____

_____

_____

_____

_____

_____

_____

_____

Day 8
Hello

Pray Continually.
1 Thessalonians 5:17 (NIV)

In the same way, the Spirit helps us in our weakness.
We do not know what we ought to pray for, but the
Spirit himself intercedes for us through wordless groans.
Romans 8:26 (NIV)

In my Adele voice: "Hello! It's me!" That is me every day when I go to God. Sometimes it's me on my knees, sometimes it's me in my car, and sometimes it's me at work. Even when I have nothing to say, He hears me. Prayer is not a practice; it is a conversation with your best friend. It is merely your conversation with God. This is simply your worship. When it comes to prayer, it doesn't have to be drawn out or "preacher sounding"; it is your sincere words to God. The Bible says in Romans 8:26 that if you don't know how or what to pray, it doesn't matter; He does our praying in and for us. He makes prayers out of our wordless sighs and our aching groans. Can you believe that even when I suck my teeth and sigh heavily, He understands and prays for me when I can't? How awesome is that? Don't get focused on setting up time to pencil Him into your busy schedule. Include Him in your day-to-day life. Talk to Him throughout the day. It is not talking to yourself—I just freed someone right there. Talk to Him out loud! Never stop praying!

Journal Prompt: What are some things you have been praying about? What comes to mind when you start your conversations with God?

Virtuous Prayer: Lord, thank you for blessing me with the privilege of having a conversation with God. Understanding that I have access to you constantly is something I don't abuse. So whether I have something to say or not, I am coming to you first with a sense of gratitude for connecting with me. You have so many people that can occupy your time, but you always make time for me! I pray and talk to you every day of my life. Amen.

_____

_____

_____

_____

_____

_____

_____

_____

_____

_____

_____

_____

_____

_____

_____

_____

_____

_____

_____

_____

_____

_____

_____

_____

_____

_____

_____

_____

_____

_____

_____

_____

_____

_____

_____

_____

_____

_____

_____

_____

_____

_____

_____

_____

Day 9
Believe

Now faith is confidence in what we hope for
and assurance about what we do not see.
Hebrews 11:1 (NIV)

As our walk with God continues to grow, it is a constant reminder to believe and have faith in Him. In the past couple of days, our belief process has changed when it comes to Christ. Once we were weary, and now we have full confidence in the Lord. Romans 15:13 (ESV) says, "May the God of hope fill you with all joy and peace in believing, so that by the power of the Holy Spirit you may abound in hope." Certain things I used to believe God for were to have a family and to walk into my purpose. It is now 2024; I have a beautiful family, and here I am with this devotional as my purpose.

We will tap into purpose more in the next devotional, but the latest thing that I'm believing God for is complete submission to Him and building disciples in my children. I'm believing in Christ for total submission because, again, I've straddled the fence long enough. Now it's time to surrender all. The people-pleasing—or even self-pleasing—is behind me now. I just want to be obedient. I encourage you today, whatever it is you are believing God for— even if it is a newfound relationship with Him—be patient. Just know that we serve a God who will take care of you. James 4:10 (ESV) says, "Humble yourselves before the Lord, and He will exalt you." Just have faith and believe in Him!

Journal Prompt: What do you believe about God?

Virtuous Prayer: Lord, thank you for believing in me. Thank you for selecting me to be a part of your family. Because of you, I have so much faith in me, and I have confidence in you. I believe all things are possible with you. With you, I can do exceeding and abundantly above all that I could ask or think. My belief in you is demonstrated through my obedience. With you and me, we are unstoppable. Amen!

_____

_____

_____

_____

_____

_____

_____

_____

_____

_____

_____

_____

_____

_____

_____

_____

_____

_____

_____

Day 10
Faithful to You

Do not be afraid of what you are about to suffer. I tell you,
the devil will put some of you in prison to test you, and you will
suffer persecution for ten days. Be faithful, even to the point of
death, and I will give your life as your victor's crown.
Revelation 2:10 (NIV)

When I was in seminary, I did an assignment on Thomas the Apostle, also known as Doubting Thomas. For those that don't know, he initially doubted the resurrection of Jesus Christ but later confessed his faith once he saw the wounds of Jesus. I was so fascinated by him because he was able to spread the gospel to India and China. It was because of his faith that he became a martyr. I remember in class, the professor asked if our faith in God would waver if we faced death in His name. Of course, we saw it with Peter, and he denied Christ three times. So there is evidence of self-doubt in us. It was interesting that in class everyone agreed their faith would never waver. Even I agreed.

However, as I began to dwell on it, I began to think, "What if?" We've seen news reports of people being murdered for believing in Christ. I remember, years ago there was a mass shooting, and the shooter asked the victims before killing them if they believed in God. When I read this scripture, I'm comforted because Christians do face persecution sometimes, but they remain strong and have faith in God. Even Jesus Himself was persecuted, but He never wavered. A true example is Job. He lost everything and still never wavered. No matter how hard life gets, always stand ten toes down! Even at the end, always look to the heavens! Always know there is something greater on the other side.

Journal Prompt: What are some areas that you doubt God in? What steps are you willing to take to change your doubts?

Virtuous Prayer: Lord, I want to be faithful to you! I want to be your friend, like the scripture says. I want to have unwavering faith in you, that even if I am confronted with death, I will choose you always. The true victory is meeting you, and that is what I aspire to do. God, I thank you for your Word and that I can be comforted when having moments of doubt. I love you to eternity. Amen!

_____
_____
_____
_____
_____
_____
_____
_____
_____
_____
_____
_____
_____
_____
_____
_____

Principle #3: Time and Purpose

She brings him good, not harm, all the days of her life.
She selects wool and flax and works with eager hands.
She is like the merchant ships, bringing her food from afar.
She gets up while it is still night; she provides food for her
family and portions for her female servants.
Proverbs 31:12–15 (NIV)

I make known the end from the beginning,
from ancient times, what is still to come.
I say, "My purpose will stand,
and I will do all that I please."
Isaiah 46:10 (NIV)

WE made it! We survived our very own personal wilderness. For some, it has been ten long days; for others, like me, it has been decades. Close to the end of 2022, I was starting to walk out what our next principle would be, which is time and purpose. When you have done the inner work and fully immersed yourself in the Lord, it is only right that your outer work reflects that. So, these next principles reflect what God has already done on the inside of us. Remember, we are not the same people as when we started this devotional. At this point, we are virtuous women and now waiting for our godly task on Earth.

Over the next couple of days, start thinking about your strengths and talents. Start asking how you can be used by Him in your daily life. What are you investing your time in currently? Keep all of these things in mind as we explore tapping into your purpose.

Day 11
#CommissionChallenge

Then the eleven disciples went to Galilee, to the mountain
where Jesus had told them to go. When they saw him, they wor-
shiped him; but some doubted. Then Jesus came to them and
said, "All authority in heaven and on earth has been given to me.
Therefore go and make disciples of all nations, baptizing them
in the name of the Father and of the Son and of the Holy Spirit,
and teaching them to obey everything I have commanded you.
And surely I am with you always, to the very end of the age."
Matthew 28:16–20 (NIV)

We currently live in a time where all we see is TikTok challenges. Some of the most recent popular challenges
include the #cuffitchallenge by Beyoncé and my favorite, #yam-
schallenge, by Fetty Wap. Every time you get on social media,
there is a new challenge happening. Whether it's singing, danc-
ing, or doing a crazy stunt, people are doing it and posting it.

Thinking about society in general, we are so prone to do
anything for likes and attention. However, when it comes to
witnessing for your faith, it's crickets. I got saved when I was
young, and my parents used to tell me that no matter what you
do in your life, your main mission is to tell someone about Jesus. They showed me this scripture in Matthew. To this day,
I remember witnessing to my best friend, and she committed
herself to the Lord that day. I told myself I could go to heaven
because my main goal was to at least get one. Then, as I got

older, it became people I randomly came across, people at my job, and now my children.

When it comes to your children, discipleship starts in the home. I make a conscious effort to plant seeds in my children. In my home, our family has a mission statement. It reads, "The Holleys will show love to each other through the traits of tenderness, mercy, grace, forgiveness, and gentleness. Our words are uplifting, our tone encouraging. We will think of each other before ourselves. These characteristics will be carried outside our home as we share the love of Jesus Christ with those around us." Even with my family, our mission is to demonstrate the fruit of the Spirit at home so we can demonstrate it outside of the home. It always comes back to sharing the gospel.

If you ever wonder what your purpose is, it starts here. You are here on this earth to spread the good news. You are a living testimony, and it is supposed to be shared. We are to build community and support those that are struggling with things we overcame. Your testimony will save a life literally and eternally. So do you accept the #CommissionChallenge today?

Journal Prompt: As Christians, we know the Great Commission. What are some ways you can execute this challenge?

Virtuous Prayer: Lord, I accept the challenge of the Great Commission. If I never had a purpose, I understand now. My purpose in life is to share the good news about you. I thank you for revealing yourself in that. I was born to fulfill this mission. My prayer today is for you to show me how to do this through my skills, conversations, and passion to bring as many souls as possible to you. Thank you for choosing me. Amen.

Day 12

Irreplaceable

For the gifts and the calling of God are irrevocable.
Romans 11:29 (ESV)

My favorite line from the song "Irreplaceable" by Beyoncé is "Don't you ever for a second get to thinking you're irreplaceable." Now, I know the song refers to a man being replaced at any minute, but when it comes to our relationship with God, He is irreplaceable, just like the gifts that God has placed inside of you; they will never go away.

I say that because here I am, thirty-six-years old, and this vision of *The Reconstruction of a Virtuous Woman* started in 2008. As much as I tried to ignore it and do other things, God kept bringing it to my remembrance. Despite my career changes, my passion is being creative. I can write, produce, and edit a show if I put effort into it. I know that is something only God could give me the ability to do. When I was in high school, I created a music video. To this day, I envision music video concepts because I know it is embedded in me. I have so many ideas that I want to do, and this devotional is the first of many. Just know that your gifts are here to stay. It is up to you to use them.

Journal Prompt: What are some gifts or passions that keep you up at night? What is holding you back from tapping into your gifts?

Virtuous Prayer: Lord, I thank you for the gifts you planted inside of me. If I'm unaware of my gifts, I pray that you will reveal them to me. Lord, I'm so amazed that when creating me, you gave me gifts that make me unique. I love you for creating me to execute your plan of bringing as many souls to you as I can. My life is for a purpose, and I will serve my purpose with the gifts you gave me. Keep my gifts resonating inside me if you see me slipping away; let it be my motivator to live for you. In Jesus' name, amen.

_____

_____

_____

_____

_____

_____

_____

_____

_____

_____

_____

_____

_____

_____

_____

_____

_____

_____

_____

_____

_____

_____

_____

_____

_____

_____

_____

_____

_____

_____

_____

_____

_____

_____

_____

_____

_____

_____

_____

_____

_____

_____

_____

Day 13
Put It on Wax!

And the LORD answered me, and said, "Write the vision, and
make it plain upon tables, that he may run that readeth it.
Habakkuk 2:2 (KJV)

We all know that everything starts with an idea or vision. Today I want you to find ways to write your vision or ideas for
the year. There are so many ways to put your ideas on wax. Every
year I either do a vision board or attend a vision board party. This
is how I start my year, and I always go back to it during the mid-
dle and end of the year to see if I accomplished some of my goals.

For this devotional, I wrote out the titles and scriptures
months before writing the actual book. Writing the first few ele-
ments gave me an outline, and what's funny is, I wrote this par-
ticular devotion on a random piece of paper. I kept it in my purse
every day as I wrote. The same paper is torn up a little bit, but I'm
determined to remind myself of how long I've been writing this
and how important it is for this book to come out. Whatever you
write, let it be a guide and motivator. Enough talking...it is time
to pray and write.

Journal Prompt: Write from your heart! (Freestyle it.)

Virtuous Prayer: Lord, thank you for giving me the time and
space to write out your vision for my life. Please reveal it to me
so I can write it down plain as day. Lord, help me to strategize

dates and time frames to execute the final goal. Lord, block all the distractions, both seen and unseen, that will hinder my vision. I can do all things through Christ that strengthens me. I know, whatever vision you give me, it can be obtained. This is the beginning of what could be great and prosperous for the Kingdom. I love you, Father! Amen!

_____

_____

_____

_____

_____

_____

_____

_____

_____

_____

_____

_____

_____

_____

_____

_____

_____

_____

_____

_____

_____

_____

_____

_____

_____

_____

_____

_____

_____

_____

_____

_____

_____

_____

_____

_____

_____

_____

_____

_____

_____

_____

_____

_____

_____

_____

_____

_____

_____

_____

Day 14

Just Do It!

This is why it is said:
"Wake up, sleeper,
rise from the dead,
and Christ will shine on you."

Be careful, then, how you live—not as unwise but as wise,
making the most of every opportunity,
because the days are evil.
Therefore do not be foolish,
but understand what the Lord's will is.
Ephesians 5:14–17 (NIV)

cannot take credit for this, as today's message came from Pastor Dwight Riddick from St. Mark Missionary Baptist Church in Portsmouth, Virginia. My sorority sister, Sondrea, sent me this sermon after I told her I had stopped writing this devotional. I had expressed to her that I couldn't write this book and wasn't qualified. I had fears about people's opinions of this book. She sent me this sermon, and I'm telling you like she told me: "Just Do It!"

Do it afraid! Be obedient to what God is speaking to you. Don't let the devil stop you from accomplishing what God has told you to do. Understand that opportunity comes with opposition. All your fears and insecurities are keeping you from releasing what God is telling you to do, because the devil saw the impact of what your gift is going to do for the kingdom.

As I was hit hard, things in my life started to unravel. I realized my life became harder when I stopped writing it. You are going to be met with some opposition, but don't let that stop you. The scripture says to make the most of every opportunity because the days are evil. Understand that we may fall on some dark times but God has called you to be a light. Seize every opportunity to live for God and carry out your purpose for God. In the words of Nike, "Just Do It!"

Journal Prompt: How will you seize the opportunity today to live out your purpose?

Virtuous Prayer: Lord, I pray to do whatever you ask me to do. I pray you remove the fears and anxieties. I pray you remove any negative thoughts hindering my call. God, I'm aware that every opportunity is met with opposition. I'm aware that you've equipped me to endure. I know that whatever I'm called to do will come to pass. I know you've got my back! In Jesus' name, amen!

_____

_____

_____

_____

_____

_____

_____

_____

_____

_____

_____

_____

_____

_____

_____

_____

_____

_____

_____

_____

_____

_____

_____

_____

_____

_____

_____

_____

_____

_____

_____

_____

_____

_____

_____

_____

Day 15

Always on Time

There is a time for everything,
and a season for every activity under the heavens:
a time to be born and a time to die,
a time to plant and a time to uproot,
a time to kill and a time to heal,
a time to tear down and a time to build,
a time to weep and a time to laugh,
a time to mourn and a time to dance,
a time to scatter stones and a time to gather them,
a time to embrace and a time to refrain from embracing,
a time to search and a time to give up,
a time to keep and a time to throw away,
a time to tear and a time to mend,
a time to be silent and a time to speak,
a time to love and a time to hate,
a time for war and a time for peace.
Ecclesiastes 3:1–8 (NIV)

Let me stop and say, if you made it to this day, just look at this new version of you. I am so proud of you! Remember, at this point, God has probably created an album dedicated to you because He is singing your name with praise. Just think about the work you have done over these past fifteen days! You stripped yourself to your raw nakedness, and you transformed into this beautiful butterfly. With your transformation comes your destination, and with that, I encourage you to trust the process and the pace. There is a time for everything. As I said, it took me decades to write this devotional, but this devotional was meant to be written and shared during this time in my life. If I had written this years ago, it wouldn't have made sense, because I wasn't living right. Now I'm desperate to the point of having true reverence for God. This was delayed but never denied. Your time and season are upon you. Are you ready?

Journal Prompt: Understanding that timing is everything, how will you refrain from succumbing to the pressures of acting out of God's timing?

Virtuous Prayer: Lord, thank you for the gift of timing. I understand that I don't operate on my timing but yours. Please allow my experiences, my joys, and my lows to guide me to your perfect time to execute my call. Lord, please don't allow me to move with haste. Please help me understand that you are with me on this journey. I pray and accept the things that I cannot change, need the courage to change the things I can, and the wisdom to know the difference.

Day 16
Jabez's Prayer

Jabez cried out to the God of Israel, "Oh, that you would bless
me and enlarge my territory! Let your hand be with me, and
keep me from harm so that I will be free from pain."
And God granted his request.
1 Chronicles 4:10 (NIV)

When I was in college, one of my girlfriends gave me a book called *The Prayer of Jabez* by Bruce Wilkinson. I remember her telling me she read this book and would say this prayer every day when she woke up in the morning. She warned that once you pray this, God will answer in such a way.

So I started reading this book and was blown away by the story about Jabez. This Old Testament prayer demonstrates that when we go to God, we should not treat Him like a genie in a bottle. Instead, we should call upon God to help us accomplish His promises! Jabez's name came from the pain that his mother endured while she was in labor.

In the first verse, you see that he cries out to God. Jabez is showing vulnerability. This verse shows you how to start your prayer. He first acknowledged that God is the Head and Lord of his life. When Jabez prays "bless me," he understands that all blessings come from God. When he prays about enlarging his territory, he is not talking about land or wealth; he is talking about kingdom impact. He is talking about his faith being increased and the generations knowing about Christ. Lastly, he prays, "Let your hand be with me," understanding that God will never leave him or forsake him. He knows that he has God's protection over his life. When you understand this prayer, you will understand the true reward is holiness and conquering the great commission.

As we end this section on time and purpose, I hope you realize His calling is bigger than yours. Be prepared to go to unfamiliar territory, but just know God is equipping you and will be with you along the way.

Journal Prompt: How does Jabez's prayer change your outlook on prayer?

Virtuous Prayer: Memorize Jabez's prayer.

_____

_____

_____

_____

_____

_____

_____

_____

_____

_____

_____

_____

_____

_____

_____

_____

_____

_____

_____

_____

_____

_____

_____

_____

_____

_____

_____

_____

_____

_____

_____

_____

_____

_____

_____

_____

_____

_____

_____

_____

_____

_____

_____

_____

_____

Principle #4: Nurture Relationships

She speaks with wisdom,
and faithful instruction is on her tongue.
She watches over the affairs of her household
and does not eat the bread of idleness.
Her children arise and call her blessed;
her husband also, and he praises her.
Proverbs 31:26–28 (NIV)

We are now on the fourth principle. For the first three principles, we did a lot of work within, and it was challenging. At this point, the inner work is reflected outwardly. If you have made it to this point, you will begin to see changes in your relationships, your appearance, and the continuation of applying these principles to your everyday life. Kudos to you! The old version of you is in the rearview mirror. The more you start seeing yourself the way God sees the Proverbs 31 woman, you will see that your relationships will start to change.

When I started my journey, I only wanted to be around people who poured into me. At the time, I was single, and I stopped entertaining certain men. I was practicing celibacy, so I deleted all the dating apps and just trusted God. I was intentional about everything in my life. This was the part where I strongly felt whole within myself. I was navigating through life with purpose. My singleness was with purpose, the way I handled friendships was with purpose, and the way I conducted myself at work was with purpose.

Over the next few days, start assessing your relationships. Ask the people around you what they think of you. If you are unsure, ask your best friend, Jesus.

Day 17
Savannah James

Her children arise and call her blessed;
her husband also, and he praises her.
Proverbs 31:28 (NIV)

I know you're wondering, who is Savannah James? Mrs. James is LeBron James's wife. I know you're thinking, what does she have to do with anything about this devotional? I started following this woman last year, and as far as celebrities go, she is the only person whose voice I've never heard. To this day, I still don't know what she sounds like. I admire her so much because even though I've never heard her speak, I've never heard anything negative about her on social media or in the press. It has always been positive. She is an amazing wife and mother. What I find most intriguing is that I always hear or read positive things spoken by her husband and her children. The most is from her husband! I never hear anything from this woman, but her family speaks so highly of her.

The scripture today reflects on that. My question to you is, what are people saying about you? There is a saying that you know what you represent in a person's life by what they call you for. I can honestly say that the closest ones to me know I'm loyal, encouraging, a good listener, and a prayer warrior. If you are single, what do your friends, siblings, or parents say about you? If you're married, what do your husband and children say about you? What common trait stands out? If anything negative comes up, you can decide what you want to do with this information. The moral of the story is, when you are no longer able to speak for yourself, what will people say on your behalf?

When I think about this, I think about social media influencer Kevin Samuels. He was known for his commentary on women and relationships, and people had a love/hate relationship with him. Whatever you felt about him, he started conversations. He passed away in May 2022, and I remember seeing all these negative comments about him; no one had anything positive to say. Again, you can agree or disagree with him, but this man was a person. He was someone's son or father. This all goes back to legacy. Today, think about how you want to show up in the world.

Journal Prompt: After having conversations with your loved ones, what common traits do you hear about yourself?

Virtuous Prayer: Father, thank you for allowing me to reach this day and empowering me to live a virtuous life in your name. I pray that as I continue to grow in you, the people around me will start to see the light in me. I pray they recognize that you gave me this joy and peace and that I don't look like yesterday or last year. I pray that as I grow in you, the closest ones to me will begin to speak well of me when I'm not around. If they praise me in front of me, let me testify that it was all because of you. In Jesus' name, amen.

Day 18
Best Friend

Therefore encourage one another and build each other up,
just as in fact you are doing.
1 Thessalonians 5:11 (NIV)

Remain in me, as I also remain in you.
No branch can bear fruit by itself; it must remain in the vine.
Neither can you bear fruit unless you remain in me.
John 15:4 (NIV)

It is a blessing that we have people to share life with. In fact, Genesis 2:18 says it is not good for man to be alone. God understands the importance of community. He even knows the dangers of isolation and how it can expose you to the devil's lies and evils. Proverbs 18:1 says (NKJV), "A man who isolates himself seeks his own desire; He rages against all wise judgment." It is extremely important to encourage one another. Encouragement can be in the form of prayer or sending scripture to one another that speaks truth and love. Building each other up shows God we all are striving for holiness and to be more like Him.

It's important to become a part of a local church for fellowship. If you don't have a church home, this is a good stepping stone to finding individuals on the same journey as you. Part of my growth was being a part of a church. When I joined Messiah Community Church in 2013, it gave me community, accountability, and devoted friends. I have friends I can call, and we pray, worship, and encourage one another. As a wife, I have my sister in Christ who speaks the truth and holds me accountable to be a better wife to my husband. I have friends praying over my children. I'm currently not in church right now, but I have friends who will get in the trenches with me and pray. I have a spouse who goes to God for counsel.

The devil has no way with you when you are protected. I challenge you today to start encouraging people around you. Speak life to them. When I couldn't encourage myself, I would get on social media and start praying for others. It made me feel so much better and gave me a life with purpose.

Journal Prompt: How will you encourage someone today?

Virtuous Prayer: Father, thank you for the people you have in my life. Whether it's my friends, family, or spouse, I thank you for having people I can share life with. Father, I pray to encourage people around me. I pray that you bring people into my life who will encourage me daily. We can help each other grow in you each day. I pray that when life gets tough, I'll have people around who will get on their knees and pray for me. I pray for fellowship and accountability to become a better me. In Jesus' name, amen.

_____

_____

_____

_____

_____

_____

_____

_____

_____

_____

_____

_____

_____

_____

_____

_____

_____

_____

_____

_____

_____

_____

_____

_____

_____

_____

_____

_____

_____

_____

_____

_____

_____

_____

Day 19

Gurl...Gossip Folks

Do not let any unwholesome talk come out of your mouths, but only what is helpful for building others up according to their needs, that it may benefit those who listen.
Ephesians 4:29 (NIV)

As we continue to encourage one another, let's be mindful of the conversations we entertain. In the past, these were some of the ugly truths about me. I was a gossiper. Chile', I was all about the tea. I lived for people's stories. I especially loved talking about people I didn't like or respect. I enjoyed anything that was said and even spread it because I didn't like them.

Well, when you become the center of everyone's gossip, it doesn't feel pretty. As I mentioned before, I used to speak badly about my ex-boyfriend and his wife. When we broke up, social media went to new heights in 2010. I saw all his and his wife's friends talking about me. Our love triangle was their focal point. I cut off a lot of people because of what they said about me. Fast forward to now, and I've had conversations with a few people but some I chose not to. However, that moment humbled me, and now I cringe when someone talks about someone else.

Back then, I was full of anger and rage. Now I've found peace and love. My conversations are all about encouragement and peace. They say to protect your peace, and refraining from gossip is protecting mine. I'm constantly checking my conversations to be better. I'm praying for the people I've talked about, wishing them well. "Minding my business and drinking my water" is my motto every day. I encourage you to speak life into people and avoid being part of conversations that don't speak to who you are as a person.

Journal Prompt: How do you filter your conversations?

Virtuous Prayer: Father, thank you for changing me for the better. Please remove me or keep me out of conversations that do not benefit my life. Please allow me to have conversations that build people up and encourage them to be like you. Father, forgive me if I have gossiped in the past. I understand that hurt people hurt people, so I want to show I have peace and happiness in my conversations. In Jesus' name, amen.

_____

_____

_____

_____

_____

_____

_____

_____

_____

_____

_____

_____

_____

_____

Day 20
Clique

Walk with the wise and become wise,
for a companion of fools suffers harm.
Proverbs 13:20 (NIV)

I know you've heard the saying, "You are the company that you keep." I've been a part of many cliques, from my childhood friends to college friends and sorority sisters. I have learned that your friends reflect where you are in life. As I mentioned previously, I was all about the tea, and I had some friends who were down for the tea and the drama.

As I've grown in my walk with God, I have seen the highs and lows of my friendships. I'm realizing now, at thirty-six, that it's okay to have a small number of friends. It's even okay that seasons change with friends and not everybody can join you in your walk. One thing I know is that God is always present. The more you read the Word, the more you want to surround yourself with similar people. I don't have new friends right now, but I'm open because I'm intentional about finding strong women in the faith that I can fellowship and have accountability with. I am grateful for the ones I have because we pray together, we don't gossip, we build each other up, and we tell each other when we're wrong.

After reading this verse, you should look at your circle and see if this is bringing you closer to God or moving you further away. I made some tough decisions, but I don't regret them because they drew me closer to Him. Choose wisely.

Journal Prompt: Do your friends bring you closer to God or pull you away?

Virtuous Prayer: Father, thank you for your words. Thank you for the people you've brought into my life and for removing the people you have removed. Lord, as I continue to walk this life, please bring people who are going to draw me closer to you. Please allow me to discern who can potentially pull me away as well. At the end of the day, I pray for fellowship and accountability to keep me on the right path.

_____

_____

_____

_____

_____

_____

_____

_____

_____

_____

_____

_____

_____

_____

_____

_____

_____

_____

_____

_____

_____

_____

_____

_____

_____

_____

_____

_____

_____

_____

_____

_____

_____

_____

_____

_____

_____

_____

_____

_____

_____

_____

_____

_____

_____

_____

Day 21

Deep Convo

My dear brothers and sisters, take note of this:
Everyone should be quick to listen, slow to speak and
slow to become angry, because human anger
does not produce the righteousness that God desires.
James 1:19–20 (NIV)

M y cousin Bryce called me the queen of deep convo. From the time we were nineteen to now in our thirties, our conversations have always been thought-provoking subjects. I know I am a talker. I can talk for hours, but once I got married, I realized I wasn't a good listener. I would hear things, but I wasn't truly listening with an open heart and mind—especially when it came to doing things the wrong way. I tuned out completely. This verse has truly helped me in my marriage. To be transparent, I haven't gotten it right all the time, but I have a foundation. As I've gotten older, I've become slow to speak, and I listen more now than ever. I used to always feel like I needed to respond, and now I'm realizing that not everything deserves a response. Be mindful of your conversations, and always listen before speaking.

Journal Prompt: In conversations, are you a listener or a hearer only?

Virtuous Prayer: Father, please allow me to be quick to listen and slow to speak. Please allow me to speak in love and not anger. Please allow me to speak about things that bear fruit and not waste. Allow my conversations to show the change and the direction that is leading to you. Amen.

_____

_____

_____

_____

_____

_____

_____

_____

_____

_____

_____

_____

_____

_____

_____

_____

_____

_____

_____

_____

_____

_____

_____

_____

_____

_____

Principle # 5: Beauty and Health

Charm is deceptive, and beauty is fleeting.
but a woman who fears the Lord is to be praised.
Proverbs 31:30 (NIV)

Ladies! We are almost at the finish line. I am so proud that you are getting to the final days. When you feel good on the inside, you want it to show outwardly. Beauty and health tie to your inside and outside. My mother always said to me, "You look how you feel." As I continued this path to reconstruction, I realized that I gained confidence because I was confident in Christ. The changes I made on the inside started to change how I felt about my appearance and my health. I don't look like what I've been through. Over the next five days, start thinking of ways to make changes to how you view yourself and how you want to feel. You are a new person. It is time to see how you feel.

Day 22

My Body

Do you not know that your bodies are temples of the
Holy Spirit, who is in you, whom you have received from God?
You are not your own; you were bought at a price.
Therefore honor God with your bodies.
1 Corinthians 6:19–20 (NIV)

Therefore, if anyone is in Christ, the new creation has come:
The old has gone, the new is here!
2 Corinthians 5:17 (NIV)

The old you is dead and gone! That is worth celebrating. You have been redeemed by the Lord and are no longer defined by the past. You are a new creature made in His image, and it is time to start making changes when it comes to your body. When the scripture refers to your body being a temple of the Holy Spirit, it means your body is a sacred place for the Holy Spirit. You should protect yourself against any harm that could come to your body.

In full transparency, when I first gave my life to Christ, I gave up smoking weed, drinking, and partying. However, I was still fornicating. Whether protected or not, my body was constantly getting UTIs, BVs, and all types of infections. I was constantly in Patient First getting antibiotics. In 2013, when I rededicated my life, I gave up everything, and I noticed a change in my mind, body, and spirit. I understood that my body was not my own and

I couldn't do whatever I wanted and still live for God. If had I continued doing that, I would have been constantly sick, tired, or even dead.

It doesn't have to be things we put into our bodies; it could also be stress and anxiety, which negatively affect our bodies. God created your body, and you cannot reach your full potential or even serve God while neglecting the proper care of your body. What is the point of having education, talent, and gifts if your body is not at its full capacity to complete tasks well?

In my thirties, I'm really starting to take care of my body and watch what I eat. Keep me in prayer as far as exercising, but it's about serving God and being here for my family as well. I encourage you, over the next few days, to start removing things that could be detrimental to your health and spirit.

Journal Prompt: Understanding that your body is where the Holy Spirit dwells, what are some things that you are going to remove to keep it sacred?

Virtuous Prayer: Father God, thank you for your Word. Thank you for giving me the understanding that my body is not my own. It was paid for by the blood of Jesus Christ. God, remove the toxins from my life. God, help me to have self-control and stop things that are not of you. Remind me of the bigger picture and that I'm a vessel to do your will. I thank you for redeeming me and making me a new creature in you. In Jesus' name, amen.

_____

_____

_____

_____

_____

_____

_____

_____

_____

_____

_____

_____

_____

_____

_____

_____

_____

_____

_____

_____

_____

_____

_____

_____

_____

_____

_____

_____

Day 23

Free

Dear friend, I pray that you may enjoy good health and that all
may go well with you, even as your soul is getting along well.
3 John 1:2 (NIV)

This scripture is part of my husband's and my mission statement for our business. We started Home Helpers Elite, which
is a home care agency created to provide elite care to our clients
in the comfort of their homes. The clients we serve are the el-
derly; the homebound; the terminally, chronically, and/or acute-
ly ill; and the physically and/or mentally challenged. With our
services, we want them to maximize their engagement, indepen-
dence, and health.

In the verse, John is praying that not only are we blessed
physically but also spiritually. How freeing is it that God wants
you to prosper both spiritually and physically? He wants you to
do well. I want you to do well. In one of Destiny's Child's songs,
called "Free," the lyrics say, "Ain't no feeling like being free when
your mind is made up and your heart's in the right place." It is
freeing to give all your cares to God and know He is doing everything for your good. He wants you to do well in all aspects
of your life. No matter what you struggle with or what you're going through, God wants to see you doing well. Today, be free in
Christ, and go and enjoy your life!

Journal Prompt: What is your definition of being free?

Virtuous Prayer: Thank you, God, for giving me the understanding that you want me to do well both spiritually and physically. God, I pray that whatever struggles come into my life, I have the freedom to know that you will take care of it. Thank you, God, for the freedom of having a way out. Before you, I didn't know, but now I do. I understand that I am not in bondage to my sins, my thoughts, or people's opinions. I am your child and will be blessed all the days of my life. In Jesus' name, amen.

_____

_____

_____

_____

_____

_____

_____

_____

_____

_____

_____

_____

_____

_____

_____

_____

_____

_____

_____

_____

_____

_____

_____

_____

_____

_____

_____

_____

_____

_____

_____

_____

_____

_____

_____

_____

_____

_____

_____

_____

_____

_____

_____

_____

_____

Day 24
Beauty Is Her Name

Your beauty should not come from outward adornment,
such as elaborate hairstyles and the wearing of gold jewelry or
fine clothes. Rather, it should be that of your inner self,
the unfading beauty of a gentle and quiet spirit,
which is of great worth in God's sight.
1 Peter 3:3–4 (NIV)

Hands down, Dru Hill's "Beauty" is my favorite love song. I may be a little biased because they are from my hometown, but every time the beat drops, their level of tenderness and tone show the gentleness and love of the woman they are describing.

When we think of beauty, the world's standard and God's definition are different. The world focuses on your outward appearance, and the world's most convincing consumer is a woman. Ladies, we are spending money on clothes, hair, makeup, and even plastic surgery to make ourselves beautiful or appealing to our counterparts. However, as we grow older, our beauty starts to fade. When beauty starts to fade, what do we have left?

In this scripture, Peter is encouraging women to focus on their conduct and character. He is saying beauty is within. The most interesting part is that he's saying women don't focus on what God deems valuable. God values having a gentle and quiet spirit. To develop your inner beauty, you must acquire the fruit of the Spirit, which is love, joy, peace, patience, kindness, goodness, faithfulness, gentleness, and self-control—and in some versions, also modesty, continency, and chastity.

These qualities hold value to God but are also what every husband desires to see in his wife. Whether you're single or married, understanding these qualities honors the Lord, and no amount of make-up or hair extensions will develop these characteristics. Expensive clothes won't compensate for a mean, jealous, spiteful, or bitter attitude. No perfume can mask an unforgiving heart, and no amount of jewelry can embellish a selfish woman. Today, let us identify beauty from within because that's ultimately what God sees.

Journal Prompt: A gentle and quiet spirit is exceedingly rare for women today. Why do think that is?

Virtuous Prayer: God, thank you for your Word. Thank you for the truth in your Word. I understand that beauty is fleeting but my character lives forever. Help me to adapt to the fruit of the Spirit. Help me to have a gentle and quiet spirit. Help me understand that this is not about weakness but about strength and confidence in the Lord. In Jesus' name, amen.

_____

_____

_____

_____

_____

_____

_____

_____

Day 25
Dependent Women

She is more precious than rubies; nothing you desire can compare with her. Long life is in her right hand; in her left hand are riches and honor. Her ways are pleasant ways, and all her paths are peaceful. She is a tree of life to those who take hold of her; those who hold her fast will be blessed.

Proverbs 3:15–18 (NIV)

I also want the women to dress modestly, with decency and propriety, adorning themselves, not with elaborate hairstyles or gold or pearls or expensive clothes, but with good deeds, appropriate for women who profess to worship God.

1 Timothy 2:9–10 (NIV)

Let's continue yesterday's topic of beauty. When we talk about the subject of clothing, I have learned that a truly independent woman becomes that way by her true dependence on God. Her being dependent brings strength and confidence. It shows in the work that she creates. It shows her servanthood.

Before I gave myself to the Lord, my appearance was very sexual. I thought it would make me feel good about myself and attract men. When I drew closer to the Lord, I realized none of that stuff mattered. I attracted my husband not because of my appearance but because of my values. That was a pure reflection of where I was spiritually. The concept of "less is more" became truer to me than ever before. As far as clothing, I show less of my body now, but I still demand attention when I walk into a room. Reading these scriptures showed me that since God highly values me, I should conduct myself at a higher standard. I'm setting an example for my daughters and my son. It's not about the clothes; it's how you want to be distinguished in the world. I want people to see God in me. I encourage you to show the light in you!

Journal Prompt: As you come into Christ, are you really an independent woman?

Virtuous Prayer: Father God, thank you that I can depend on you. I understand that all I've acquired isn't because of me but from you. Thank you for adding value to my life. In Jesus' name, amen.

_____

_____

_____

_____

_____

_____

_____

_____

_____

_____

_____

_____

_____

_____

_____

_____

Day 26

Mirrors

So God created mankind in his own image,
in the image of God he created them;
male and female he created them.
Genesis 1:27 (NIV)

Wow! We are five days away from completing our journey to reconstructing our lives into being virtuous women. To wrap up our last day on the principle of beauty and health, I want to think about this scripture and the word "reflection." This word has so many definitions. It could be a serious thought or consideration; it could also be the image you see in a mirror.

When I think about this scripture and how we were created in God's image, I think of a mirror. When I look in the mirror and see my reflection staring back at me, I view Christ staring back at me. I take inventory of how I can mirror my life to His. I understand that I'm flawed, but a lot of my decision making and how I conduct myself should reflect Christ.

As humans, we all struggle with this, but understand that we all come from the same Creator. We have choices every day to make to live right. What better example to mirror your life on than the way that Jesus lived? I always say if I could respond like Jesus, I would be all right. If I had a level of patience like Him, I would be great. I challenge you every single day to mirror your life like Christ. Even when adversity comes, have a posture like Christ. I know it's hard, but I dare you to try. As I am uplifting you, I'm uplifting myself in this area. If we are Christians, we are Christ-like, right?

Journal Prompt: What are some ways that you can mirror Jesus?

Virtuous Prayer: Thank you, God, for setting the example in Jesus. Jesus, thank you for being the way, the truth, and the life. Thank you, God, for creating me. I pray to reflect Christ in such a way that it brings people to Him. Let me walk and talk like Christ. In Jesus' name, amen.

_____

_____

_____

_____

_____

_____

_____

_____

_____

_____

_____

_____

_____

_____

_____

_____

_____

_____

_____

_____

_____

_____

_____

_____

_____

_____

_____

_____

_____

_____

_____

_____

_____

_____

_____

_____

_____

_____

_____

_____

_____

_____

_____

_____

_____

_____

_____

_____

_____

_____

The B-Side

As I write this, it is now November 2023, and a lot has changed since I first began writing this devotional journey. I started writing this in January 2022 with a completion date of June, just shy of my thirty-seventh birthday. From July 2022 until October 22, 2023, I was privately taking care of my mom, who was battling stage four gallbladder cancer. In April 2023, her cancer took a turn for the worse, and I quit my job and moved my mother into my home with my family for five months. Those five months consisted of going back and forth to the doctors and in and out of hospitals, not to mention I gave birth to my son, Isaiah, in July. A song that comes to mind to describe that time is Whitney Houston's "I Didn't Know My Own Strength." During those five months, my mother and I spent time together and had the opportunity to reintroduce ourselves to one another. Somedays we had a ball doing laundry and watching *Power*. Other days we argued a lot. Through the good and bad, God allowed us to have time.

If you haven't caught on by now, my mother, Linda Pickens, passed away in October 2023. Her funeral was on November 1. It is now November 9, my dad's birthday, and I have started writing again. What is interesting is how this came about. My mother moved to Maryland at the end of September to live with my brother. My mother was adamant about moving up there. At the time, I didn't want her to go, but I understood. When she left, I was jobless and undecided about applying for jobs again. My husband and I had started a home health agency in June 2022, and my husband told me I didn't have to go back to work but could just focus on growing the business. Even though that sounded good, I kept asking God, "What is my purpose?"

There were moments when I felt frustrated, and then there were moments I felt I had great ideas in the works. I started brainstorming different entrepreneurial ventures. Each idea was great, but I always felt like I was missing something. Every day leading up to today, I prayed, asking God to reveal my purpose. Each day, I would create and research potential business opportunities. Today I thought I had found the right business venture. I decided to write my business model for a co-working space that is pet friendly. I thought to myself, "I've finally got it." I went from wanting to own a pet franchise, to wanting a co-working space, to doing both. My mind was overloaded that day.

Suddenly a soft voice told me to go to YouTube and type "Anita Phillips." I typed the name, and the first video that popped up was called "Decision Tree." I watched it, nodded, and agreed. My son was crying while I was watching. As the sermon was about to end, Dr. Phillips said, "There is someone watching this online who should be doing this." She pointed to the altar. She said, "You are called to ministry and trying to talk yourself out of it." PAUSE! I paused, and God started showing me a sequence of events. He brought it all back to me and this computer.

So here I am! I left off at the last five days of this devotional. At first, I was going to write a whole new devotional, but God told me to keep writing this one because He wants me to know that He's still doing the work. This is an ongoing process. Where I was spiritually back then is not where I am today. Staying true to the theme, these last five days connect with some of the music that I played a lot in 2023. We left off at mirroring Jesus, and now we are ending with the reverence of Christ. The scripture you will reflect on these last few days is Proverbs 31:30. It states, "...a woman who fears the Lord is to be praised." The key phrase is "fears the Lord."

At my mother's funeral, the pastor who gave the eulogy preached from John 14:1–6 (NIV). The scripture says, "Do not let your hearts be troubled. You believe in God; believe also in me. My Father's house has many rooms; if that were not so, would I have told you that I am going there to prepare a place for you? And if I go and prepare a place for you, I will come back and take you to be with me so that you also may be where I am. You know the way to the place where I am going. Thomas said to him, 'Lord, we don't know where you are going, so how can we know the way?' Jesus answered, 'I am the way and the truth and the life. No one comes to the Father except through me.'"

As much as I had read and memorized this scripture, it took on a whole new meaning after my mother passed. The word "preparation" was the overall theme of the message. So as we conclude this devotional, I want all of you to know that pursuing God and choosing to live for God on this side of heaven will allow God to make room for you in heaven. Whether you stumble or life is great, always keep your eyes and heart connected to Jesus. Keep following Him, and He will lead you to the Promised Land. These last five days will focus on Jesus Himself.

Day 27
Good Good

"Why do you ask me about what is good?" Jesus replied.
"There is only One who is good. If you want to enter life,
keep the commandments."
Matthew 19:17 (NIV)

The singer Usher had an amazing year in 2023. From his residency in Las Vegas to his announcement of performing at the Super Bowl, everything seems "Good Good" with him. As I reflect on my life, things are changing for my good. The business we started last year is growing, and soon our forever home will be built. Everything is looking up.

However, as I think about everything being good, I think back to the scripture in Matthew 19. In verse 16, it says, "Just then a man came up to Jesus and inquired, 'Teacher, what good thing must I do to obtain eternal life?'" It was in reading verse 17 that I realized we as a people emphasize the word "good." "I'm a good person!" "I feel good!" We have our own definitions of what *good* is. But in this scripture, Jesus acknowledges that only God is good. To experience eternal life, we must go to Him to understand what is truly good. Mark 8:36 (NIV) says, "What good is it for someone to gain the whole world, yet forfeit their soul?" The purpose of this verse is to point out that man's goodness is imperfect and we cannot be good enough to gain eternal life on our own.

When things start to look up for you, keep your eyes on the prize. The true reward is being good on this side and the other side of life! I tell my daughter all the time, "You are too pretty to go to hell!" So, ladies, you are too precious and valuable to go down in the end. Let that marinate for a minute.

Journal Prompt: Check the temperature. Are you good?

Virtuous Prayer: Lord, thank you for being so good to me. Thank you for dying on the cross for my sins so I can have eternal life. I utterly understand that goodness in my life only comes from you. I ask you to lead me according to your will so I can join you in heaven. In Jesus' name, amen!

_____

_____

_____

_____

_____

_____

_____

_____

_____

_____

_____

_____

_____

_____

_____

_____

_____

Day 28
Keep It Breezy

Brothers and sisters, I do not consider myself yet to have
taken hold of it. But one thing I do: Forgetting what is behind
and straining toward what is ahead, I press on toward
the goal to win the prize for which God has
called me heavenward in Christ Jesus.
Philippians 3:13–14 (NIV)

I was scrolling on Instagram and stumbled across a post about
singer Chris Brown. At the height of Usher going to the Super
Bowl, there was also the conversation of Chris Brown doing a
Super Bowl. The singer responded, saying they would not let
him perform. As I was reading it, I saw many comments relating
to his past regarding his ex-girlfriend, singer Rihanna. The comments were saying he didn't deserve it, and people were wondering why he was still performing. They called him a woman
beater. You name it, they said it.

I started to empathize with him because it reminded me of
when I started my walk with God and people had nasty things to
say about me. To this day, I remember a guy telling me nobody
was going to want me. I was called all kinds of names. There are
still people who see me in that light. Now a wife and a mother,
they can't get past my old life.

I say to you, ladies, who are new creatures in Christ, as you
begin to walk in a new light, people will remind you of your past.
They will try to tempt you to resort to your old habits and behavior.

Keep It Breezy   101

Some will try to bring you down and say that you are not capable of this new life. But I'm here to tell you today that the devil is a liar! The devil only pulls things from our past because he can't pull from our future. So continue to press forward and be heavenward because, just like Chris Brown, no one can take away your gifts and talents. That is why he is still standing and so will you!

Journal Prompt: In your new walk with God, have some things from the past come up? If so, how did you respond?

Virtuous Prayer: Lord, thank you for forgetting my past and creating a new path in my life. Lord, if my past is presented in my future, please remind me where I was and where I'm headed. Please allow me to keep my mind and my heart on you. Amen.

_____

_____

_____

_____

_____

_____

_____

_____

_____

_____

_____

_____

_____

_____

_____

_____

_____

_____

_____

_____

_____

_____

_____

_____

_____

_____

_____

_____

_____

_____

_____

_____

_____

_____

_____

_____

_____

_____

_____

_____

Day 29

Water

But whoever drinks the water I give them will never thirst.
Indeed, the water I give them will become in them
a spring of water welling up to eternal life.
John 4:14 (NIV)

Whoever believes in me, as Scripture has said,
rivers of living water will flow from within them.
John 7:38 (NIV)

As you probably heard, 2023 was the year of the Afrobeats. Music was filled with African culture. Everyone from Drake to Chris Brown, Justin Bieber, and even Beyoncé joined the bandwagon of creating Afrocentric songs. But one song kept getting my attention. It was the song "Water" from Tyla. The beat is enticing—I can't lie! In all transparency, I popped my butt in the mirror. LOL! However, there is a line in the song where she says, "Can you snatch my soul from me?" I was like, "What?"

At that moment, I thought about Jesus being my water. When it comes to my life, He snatches my soul. I was hooked the minute He called my name! Stepping away from Him, I saw my life going in a different direction. I remember being at the OBGYN and the doctor telling me I would have no children if I continued to do what I was doing. Thank God I straightened up, because now I have two children and a bonus daughter. Jesus is the true water, and I never lack for anything! The Samaritan woman Jesus was talking to is my story! I stopped what I was doing and told the Good News of Jesus and what this devotional was all about. I wouldn't be here if I hadn't said yes! The life I have now was in the cards for me. So, ladies, get hydrated on Christ, and I promise you, you will never thirst again.

Journal Prompt: Describe how Jesus is the living water in your life.

Virtuous Prayer: Lord, thank you for being the living water in my life. Thank you for choosing me. I'm glad I will never thirst again. You are my true source of eternal life.

_____

_____

_____

_____

_____

_____

_____

_____

_____

_____

_____

_____

_____

_____

_____

_____

Day 30

Church Girl

He told her, "Go, call your husband and come back."
"I have no husband," she replied. Jesus said to her, "You are
right when you say you have no husband. The fact is, you have
had five husbands, and the man you now have is not your husband. What you have just said is quite true." "Sir," the woman
said, "I can see that you are a prophet."
John 4:16–19 (NIV)

I t is so crazy that as I wrap up writing this devotional, we are
headed into the end of 2023. I started this book at the beginning
of the year and am now completing it at the end. Call it divine
timing I guess! I was reading some pages earlier and thought
back to the premise of this book in reference to Beyoncé. Now,
this year a lot has been said about this woman and the tour that
she did. Everyone had something to say. You have Christians calling her demonic and saying anyone that goes to her concert is
going to hell. It was a lot. It was to the point that I didn't continue
this book. I've been praying and fasting about this topic, and to be
honest, I'm still praying. Jackie Hill Perry expressed it best. She
said that she was torn, and she lamented. She put into words
exactly what I was feeling. The one whose song kept me to the
cross was now the one I should turn away from.

The song that caused a huge fuss was the song "Church
Girl." Now, I don't like the song, but this indeed is the story of
my life. I was the girl going to church on Sundays but pop, lock,

and dropping it Monday through Saturday. It wasn't until God exposed me and my sins that I was forced to change. As I look back on my peers and things that don't align with my walk, I simply pray and change the song. We do not know how celebrities are outside of being performers, and from the words of my momma, "I don't have a heaven or hell to put you in." So with that said, all I can do is what is best for me and move accordingly. My walk is gearing more toward gospel music. In all honesty, it's still baby steps for me. I ask you to continue to pray and seek what is best for you and your walk.

Journal Prompt: Self-Inventory—What are some things that God is nudging you to stop or be aware of?

Virtuous Prayer: Father, thank you for calling me out and exposing my truths to find the truth in you. Lord, some things in life don't align with my walk. Instead of talking badly or judging, help me to simply walk away from it. In Jesus' name, amen.

_____

_____

_____

_____

_____

_____

_____

_____

_____

_____

Day 31

On My Momma

*A good person leaves an inheritance for their children's children,
but a sinner's wealth is stored up for the righteous.*
Proverbs 13:22 (NIV)

Ladies! You did it! We made it! I can't believe it. I completed this book on the last day of 2023. What a year it has been! God has stripped us and changed us from within. For me, I was blessed with my son, but I lost my mom within three months after his birth. I've experienced the beginning of life and the end of life, and all I can think about is how God was faithful the entire time.

Look back to how you started and where you are now. You are virtuous. God said that you are! You don't have to question it now. You can boldly walk in confidence because you are part of a royal priesthood. Being part of a strong lineage, it is important to spread the good news. Share this with any woman, young or old, so they may be renewed in Christ.

My mom instilled in me lessons about God, and I'm passing these down to my children. My mom also had trauma, and I must break the curse for my daughters. I *stand on business* when I say I'm ready to piss the devil off—just like you after today. Let the devil tremble because God is using you to bring more virtuous women to Him. Cheers to the new year, or should I say, new you! Happy New YOU!

Journal Prompt: It is a new you! What are your goals for the new you, and how will you execute them?

Virtuous Prayer: Lord, thank you for allowing me to finish this devotional. I finally realized that I've been a virtuous woman all along. I pray to continue growing in you and to spread the good news along my journey. I thank you for never giving up on me! I am forever grateful to you. In Jesus' name, amen.

_____

_____

_____

_____

_____

_____

_____

_____

_____

_____

_____

_____

_____

_____

_____

_____

_____

_____

_____

_____

Closing

As we conclude this thirty-one-day devotional journey, may each day's reflection serve as a stepping stone in the construction of your mind toward the virtuous woman that God intended you to be. Embrace the transformative power of faith, wisdom, and grace as you continue to build a foundation rooted in love, integrity, and purpose. Remember, the reconstruction of your mind is an ongoing process, and with each day, you will draw closer to embodying the divine virtues that reflect the beauty and strength within you. May your journey ahead be filled with God's guidance, and may you continue to walk confidently in the path of virtue, shining brightly as a testament to the transformative power of a mind aligned with God's purpose.

About the Author

Tristian Holley received Christ as her personal savior at the age of ten; She rededicated her life in February 2012. Through her intense study of the Word of God, she admired the books of Esther and Ruth. It wasn't until she read Proverbs 31 that her life changed forever.

On Facebook every Tuesday and Thursday, Tristian prays for her followers. After sharing her story one day, one of her followers reached out to her wanting to know what the process was like for living a true Christian life. Tristian felt like it was a question that most new believers or rededicated Christians ask themselves. After praying about it, she received her confirmation and *The Reconstruction of A Virtuous Woman* was born.

Unafraid to express her candid views, Tristian brings authenticity and compassion to her audience. She wants to inspire women who had been broken, depressed, angry, mistreated, misguided, abused, suicidal, and devastated with sickness and disease; be delivered, healed and victorious through Jesus Christ. Learn more about Tristian and *31 Days Towards The Reconstruction of a Virtuous Woman* at reconstructionvw.com.

Connect & Share

If you enjoyed this book, please order copies for women you know and leave a review on Amazon, Barnes & Noble, and the website where you purchased this book.

Connect with the author at
reconstructionvw.com.